Copyright © 2021 by Paul How

Bible quotations are from the Revised Standard Version, Second Catholic Edition, except when stated otherwise.

Cover by Brandon Cueto

How to be Catholic during your rebellious years

Paul How

To my two mothers, Mary and Telly

Contents

INTRODUCTION	10

ADDRESSING YOUR COMPLAINTS

1. Who Christ is to you	16
2. You're all a bunch of hypocrites!	19
3. Old Testament meanie	21
4. People during Jesus' time found Him absurd too!	24
5. What about the non-Christians?	27
6. 'Conscience is just fear of being caught'	36
7. A world of suffering	40
8. Jesus' unfair death	43

BECAUSE SCIENCE

9. BEAN	46
10. Energy	53
11. 'In this day and age'	55

CATHOLIFE

12. Brothers and sisters in Christ	58
13. Make virginity cool again	62
14. Mother Mary	65
15. Demon wrestling	69
16. Entertainment	71
17. Politics	74
18. Prayer makes the world go round	76
19. Pray for the healing of three people every night	81
20. The Bible	83
21. Sacraments	86
22. Obedience	92
23. The Philippines	97

COMING HOME

    24. My conversion   101

    25. You found Jesus; now what?   114

    26. A rebel's prayer   119

ACKNOWLEDGMENTS   120

ABOUT   121

INTRODUCTION

What do you mean my rebellious years? This isn't just a phase! If you only knew what I knew.

I recently realized that if I were to write a book on Catholicism, I would want to address those in late adolescence or early adulthood. I myself was 15 when I strayed from the Church. Ironically, it was around the time I got confirmed. And looking back, after about a year since I returned, I'm thinking of what I could have said to myself back then not just to keep me in the faith, but to actually grow in the faith. Because it's quite clear that the education I had received was insufficient. Lessons in religion class were either too boring, academic, or superficial in their treatment of the daily life of one whose eyes are being opened to the world, not necessarily to sinful pleasures, but to preoccupations that without a foundation in Christ serve to erode whatever faith had been built until then. In my case, music was the new idol. The exhilaration I got from listening and performing it seemed to make most other things dull, including the mass, which I'd always found a boring chore anyway, whose only appeal seemed to be the songs, many of which I still love. When I turned away

INTRODUCTION

from the Church, it didn't feel like a rebellion, but rather a growing out of, to better things.

And when other belief systems entered my consciousness, with *their* explanations of who or what Christ is, my impressionable self thought I was a spiritual pioneer of sorts.

Perhaps the greatest blessing of my decades-long rebelliousness is that I'm here to talk you out of yours, or to at least convince you to keep up the prayers — not just to some general 'God' figure, not just to some infinite spirit or impersonal cosmic force, but to Jesus Christ, Who has revealed Himself through the Bible. Even as you are swayed by the reasonable arguments towards paganism, even when you think Jesus was nothing more than a great teacher equivalent to Krishna or Muhammad, or even a merely symbolic myth, pray a sentence to Jesus when you can, something like, "Jesus, let me know Who You are."

I'm not very wordy, really. If I could avoid contextualizations, I do. So if you see an unfamiliar term or name, please google it yourself. It's better for us both if I get to the point, while you have all the luxury of time to search definitions and backgrounds. I'm sure you've read books where the author would just go on and on about one side issue, straying from what the book was supposed to be about. I can't guarantee I won't do that, but will try to keep it interesting at least.

The arguments for the faith contained here may not be the best ones, but I think they're what I would have had to hear as a teenager to at least give the Church another look. There are a lot of scholars I enjoy reading now, but I'm doubtful I would have even given them a chance, in my former know-it-allness.

This isn't meant to be a feel-good story, even though I try to bring good news, the best news even, to you. But even Jesus wasn't about peace *per se*, in the sense of contented agreement with one another. He came not to bring peace but a sword (Matthew 10:34). The world isn't okay as it is, and we have to be more okay with challenging others' beliefs, while being ready to defend and suffer for ours. This doesn't mean being a nitpicky troll either. It's best to leave the groundwork to God, who graces each of us with knowledge of Him as He knows best.

Maybe I don't use the word 'rebellious' in this book's title right. Given how Christian values are constantly being chipped away in society, *real* rebelliousness lies in going back to Jesus Christ. Christ is the true rebel in this age where the very idea of 'organized religion' is dismissed in favor of a supposedly more culturally dynamic and enlightened spirituality.

Although I try to reach lapsing Catholics based on my experience, I hope to shed some light on the faith to non-Catholic believers in Christ, to those

INTRODUCTION

raised in non-Christian cultures, and to atheists. But a book could only do so much. The essential thing is prayer, and the sacraments.

No one's religious life is the same as another's. Some may stray even further than I did the older they get, till they die. Some may still consider themselves Christian even though they aren't reconciled to some or many aspects of the faith. And some may never feel the need to leave, and remain devout their whole lives. I don't know your particular situation, dear reader, but you might relate to some aspects of my story anyway, so let's continue.

>   Paul How
>   QC
>   December 2020

ADDRESSING YOUR COMPLAINTS

1. Who Christ is to you

Even if you haven't been practicing your Christianity of late, you probably don't *hate* Christ. You like the general idea of "Love one another." If anything, it's the traditional teachings that have deviated from His essential message of love. It's *these* misguided followers that are dividing people with their obsolete dogma. All these rituals, and maybe even some of what was transmitted in the Bible, are the result of not getting what Jesus really meant. But *you* know what He meant, based on your life experience, and what you hear from those you admire.

The above is my impression of my attitude to Jesus during the time I wasn't particularly a fan of His, which was most of my teens all the way up to 2019 when I accepted Him into my heart again. It's actually a General Patronage version, as in my faithlessness, I didn't care what I said about Him, any more than I cared about insulting a cartoon character or the Tooth Fairy. I read Friedrich Nietzsche's 'The antichrist' *trying* to feel as indignant as poor Nietzsche about the New Testament, which according to Nietzsche promoted hatred of the world. Unable to really feel anything against these people in history, I settled for looking down on these stupid idiots in church who actually still thought the Bible was meant to be taken *literally*. They weren't supposed to waste time and gasoline to pray to a God who's all around anyway. Prayer was often just conceited wish-making and to be avoided, except for its health benefits akin to meditation. By the time I began saying terrible things about our Lord and His mother Mary, whether as a joke or in righteous anger about some important cause of the day, I thought nothing of it. They were just words. We should all be free at least to be able to say anything, right? Such 'freedom' in a very limited political sense was a component of my formula for happiness, back when I was unhappy.

Oriental religions and their counterpart, materialism disguised as science, complemented my beliefs basically throwing all faith out the window, replacing it with a world view where everything was to be explained in terms of matter, energy, and natural processes. Karma, that is, spiritual osmosis, devolved further into "Stuff just happens" or "What will be, will be."

I *felt* spiritual. I even had a mystical experience while listening to Mozart on March 1, 2002 to look back on, convincing me that I knew what it was all about, at least better than most. And if only more people knew what I knew... well, I never really explored this line of thought since I thought no one else knew as much as me, but I must have surmised that it was going to be some Utopian fantasy of peace-and-love-for-the-most-part*. But basically, I believed whatever portrayed me as *the best*, even though I really had nothing then, or at least didn't truly appreciate what I had, and I knew deep down how unhappy I was.

* Any philosophy that rejects God inevitably concedes to the imperfection of whatever high-minded system the philosopher devises. I suppose that many reject Jesus *now* because they think His arrival should have wiped out all hatred and greed in the world, and seeing this hasn't happened, yet, they go away disappointed, not acknowledging the hatred and greed they hold inside that keep them from trusting Him completely (Matthew 19:21-22).

2. You're all a bunch of hypocrites!

None of us claim perfection, though we know of it in Jesus. This doesn't mean we couldn't speak His word to each other, whenever it comes up. And the more you pray, the more He will come up in some way in your conversations. Don't let your sins stop you, particularly if you've confessed them. More on the most-important Sacrament of Reconciliation in Chapter 21.

Note that all these examples of crooks and pedophiles in the news stray from Jesus' teaching. If God is real, so is the devil, and Earth is the ground on which spiritual warfare takes place. It's not too far out to suppose that those in the Church hierarchy would be especially subject to terrible temptations.

To the extent that we still sin, we are hypocritical in evangelizing. But that shouldn't keep us from evangelizing. Quite the opposite, we should further our resolve to be obedient in all that God asks of us.

Don't let my or anybody's persistent faults keep you from what is true. Don't deprive yourself of nourishment because others don't draw from the source of nourishment as much as they claim they do.

If you truly want to know what Jesus says, you have to pay attention to the Christian doctrine. Remember that God doesn't want you to make up your mind about what constitutes the doctrine, even with the talent of reason he's given you. He wants you to say "Yes" to Him, as He has already revealed Himself in the Bible. You're not given free rein to design God as you think He should be (Genesis 3:5-6). You have to read the word He *deliberately* left for us, the Bible. You have to do things you don't think are practical, fair, or inoffensive. You have to *not* do a lot of things you don't see the harm in doing. You have to trust Him in all of this, and pray about it a lot, and pray for others whom you see no reason to pray for. You also have to trust that the gates of Hell will not prevail over the Church (Matthew 16:18), however many faults you witness in its members. Don't let smart satan (my personal term for the evil one) get to you too. In short, let God know you'll be obedient as a child.

3. Old Testament meanie

The Bible is a difficult book to say yes to. It's no wonder that it's owned more than it's read. A large part of that has to do with the Old Testament, all of which anticipates Christ's coming. But why does it have to be so long, the equivalent of more than three New Testaments? While reading the rituals for sacrifice in the first five books traditionally attributed to Moses, I want to say, "Get to the point already!"

And God's steadfast love is supposed to be eternal. Why is there so much death and punishment for sinners? It's no wonder people brush off the 'Old Testament God' in favor of the 'New Testament God,' although there really is no difference, as is made clear by Jesus, who came not to abolish the Jewish law but to fulfill it (Matthew 5:17).

He also says that what proceeds from the heart is what defiles (Matthew 15:19). Knowing this, we could look back at accounts of people being swallowed into the Earth or zapped to death for disobedience, and understand it was what was in their hearts that aggrieved the Lord. And it is only after He gives every chance to turn away from what only brings certain death, that He administers what we see as swift condemnation.

This would explain why the firstborn sons in Egypt died from the tenth plague as told in the Book of Exodus. When people are unwilling to change even after multiple signs of the error of their ways, it is the succeeding generations that suffer. This also makes sense of the violent imagery in Psalm 137:9 in which the "little ones" of the "daughter of Babylon" are to be smashed "against the rock."

We could thus see how an all-loving God, the source of all goodness, does not desire people's spiritual death, but this occurs when He is set aside. In this way, we could more easily acknowledge that the Old Testament, and not just the 'nicer, kinder' New Testament, was God's revelation of Himself to us.

God calls Himself a "jealous" God (Exodus 20:5), which does sound pretty petty on the surface. However, He speaks of being jealous not in human terms but in divine terms. It's not like God could be jealous of the good things we have in life, such as happy moments with those we love, which come from His Holy Spirit anyway.

On the other hand, He looks down on things that keep us away from His goodness, like how a parent would be concerned about their child hanging with the wrong crowd. Imagine being all-powerful and all-loving yet being shunned for the sake of satisfactions you know are fleeting and destructive to the one you love. That's the same steadfast love shown by the father in the Parable of the Prodigal Son (Luke 15:20).

Much vanquishing of foes occurs throughout the Old Testament, some of which is lawful, and some of which more plainly involves murder. God chose to bring His Son to the Jews not because of the pervasive sin in their land but in spite of it. Also remember that the Jews of the Old Testament, like other ancient peoples, were in a constant state of war, where they had to literally kill or be killed on occasion. It was a duty to protect their holy traditions and morals from outside beliefs, until the Messiah could be born.

Moses says, "Behold, I have taught you statutes and ordinances, as the Lord my God commanded me... Keep them and do them; for that will be your wisdom and your understanding in the sight of the peoples, who, when they hear all these statutes, will say, 'Surely this great nation is a wise and understanding people'." (Deuteronomy 4:5-6;9).

Whereas these Jews before the time of Christ honored God's commandments by keeping the law free of foreign Gentile influence, we Christians recognize that even our enemies are called to be saved, as we pray for them to know Jesus' love.

4. People during Jesus' time found Him absurd too!

The arrogance of our times is that we're the rational ones, while those in ancient times chalked everything up to spirits and magic. When Jesus *seemed* to multiply fish and loaves or raised the dead to life, people were just too stupid to seek a rational explanation, whereas we see a contravening of what we know as natural laws and thus know they couldn't have happened. Using the scientific method CSI-style, we in their place would have discovered something more ordinary taking place, such as the fish and loaves being hidden in people's robes the whole time. As for the dead being raised, perhaps they were just in some rare state of suspended animation, and woke up when Jesus showed up so opportunely. Anything but taking fairy tales as truth.

But seriously, it was hard to believe in Jesus' miracles, even then. That's why they were even written about. The Pharisees, upon hearing of Jesus giving sight to a blind man, refused to entertain the idea that the man really had been blind. The cured blind man, on the other hand, could only say: "One thing I know, that though I was blind, now I see" (John 9:25). He didn't understand what happened, but knew it happened anyway, from personal experience.

People during Jesus' time may not have had their theories and methodologies as we know them, but they were capable of observing scientific regularities in their daily lives. The Gospel wasn't a matter of them being too gullible to get the facts straight. When you read an account that claims something did happen (John 19:35), you can't just shut it out automatically on the assumption that these are myths, "because science."

By the way, science never really explains, it only describes. What we take as explanations are just different rephrasings of the same phenomena. If someone tells you how a carburetor works, you'll have found out *what* processes occur, but not *why* they occur. Every attempt at answering why just leads to another why back in time.

None of science pertains to what we as subjective experiencers are doing here in existence. That only comes through personal experience.

That's what prayer recognizes, and the more you pray, the more you'll see its importance. Even when scheduling conflicts happen. Even when you'd rather read or lie down. Even when it seems like an outright useless, obsolete chore. Even when running for your life. Keep praying. Prayer should be the priority of your life. You don't have to know why you should pray, but for one thing, it allows you to be grateful, to the source of gratitude itself. You're not just being grateful for gratitude's sake, as many self-help guides feel adequate; it's not. Not if you want to know true life and love. You get to recognize the truly personal dimension of it found in Jesus Christ.

If Jesus came into this world only to be misunderstood by the Evangelists, Saint Paul, the Church, and the saints, and to be understood rather by gurus from the East, New Age authors, and those brilliant enough to make sense of mere spiritual dregs that is Scripture, then there was no reason for Jesus to say, "I thank You, Father, Lord of Heaven and Earth, that You have hidden these things from the wise and understanding and revealed them to infants..." (Luke 10:21).

Which the *wise* ones would interpret as a call to humility and innocence away from dogma and anything that takes away from cleverness and rapturous exaltation. When Jesus utters words such as these, or "Let the children come to me" (Matthew 19:14), it is the *wise* ones who will reject that it pertains to Jesus specifically.

Look to your life and see how much of Jesus you allow in your life. And this indicates how you view Scripture: as exaggerated fantasy, as a mere metaphor for the human condition, *or* of God actually speaking to you at present.

Ask yourself: If God *is* love, would it be so outrageous to think He would let Himself be known to us, even reveal to us His love in His willingness to die for us, and indeed doing so?

5. What about the non-Christians?

For most of the past decade, I didn't even believe there was such a thing as religion. What we took to be religion was, to me, ways of thinking unique to each person, only placed in umbrellas of sects and cults through the broadness of language. Yet no one really thought of these spiritual figures and their teachings in exactly the same way. The proof of this was in the diversity of opinions and number of schisms within any church or branch of thought. If you told me you were a Roman Catholic, I would differentiate you from other Roman Catholics in the particular prayers and thought processes you used in the practice of your faith, where no Catholic could claim to have the exact same habits as another. Such an extremely individualistic view would not allow criticism of any of the major religions for the faults of their followers, since such faults were a matter of personal interpretation. That would be like blaming the English language for someone's murder because of the English word 'murder.'

What I now see is that I should just shut up. Christ is true, and all I have to say about language is surmounted by His presence actually uniting all people of good will. The truth of the world is God's love, His ever-abiding presence in every moment of our lives.

There is some truth to my former understanding of things. To judge people solely by the religion they proclaim to practice is prejudiced and ignorant, just as it is careless to judge someone as immoral simply because they don't profess a faith. But to refuse to tackle specific doctrine altogether because these could be interpreted in a variety of ways or sidestepped altogether, avoids the issue, in denial that cultural factors have an influence on one's actions. Playing safe in this way allows one to dismiss others' opinions as 'collectivist' while refusing to have any real opinion on the matter. We have no need for that in discussing these matters with those who think differently.

We all just have to love one another. The rest is dogmatic BS.

Except that when we discard doctrine as revealed purposefully by God, the way we show our love for one another becomes morally questionable. We have to remember that our thoughts and feelings deceive us, a lot. That's why we entrust ourselves to God by obeying His words*. When we overlook His specific commandments, it really is a way for evil to creep into our lives.

* Couldn't we be deceived into obeying Him then? If this is beginning to sound like a game of sophistry, it is. But let's allow it.

By acknowledging the uncertainty of our understanding of the world at any given time, we're not supposing everything is arbitrary or that there isn't an objective way to look at things. To suppose the world is a deception like 'The matrix' (1999) that some greater being gets a kick out of, sounds more like an individual hang-up than universal decree. With us being created in God's image, there *is* a validity to our thoughts and feelings, however distorted by original sin. It is in this validity that God allows us to know Him, in time.

One of my first definite deviations from the Church was in acccpting reincarnation, or the transferring of souls from one body to another, until through thorough spiritual discipline they are liberated from the cycle of birth and death. Or this process may continue in a universe of infinite cycles. The idea just seemed more economical, and more sensible than the idea of our souls waiting around until some last judgment.

The reason I fell for such a belief was that in my mind, the soul was nothing more than a part of nature. Thus even Man was to mimic natural forces, with reincarnation a parallel of the conservation of energy in physics.

Extending our earthly lives to a dozen or even an eternity of lifeforms doesn't reveal our spirituality more clearly. Judas lived right next to God Himself for three years, and still betrayed Him, still doubted His mercy at the very end. Would Judas have done differently in the succeeding life, or the one after that?

He wouldn't even remember his faults from before, so what's to convince him to change?

In the parable of the rich man and Lazarus (Luke 16:19-31), the rich man, upon dying, pleads for his still living brothers to be warned of the afterlife of torment, that they may repent. He is then informed that if his brothers do not already heed Moses' words, neither would they heed one coming back to life.

Reincarnation, and any hope that a sufficiently long amount of time will make for a liberated soul, is rooted in the assumption that the things that happen to us, and the way we are formed, are a matter of chance, rather than God unraveling His will with full wisdom and intent. It may be difficult to believe, what with our different lots in life, including some who die much too early, but we already have all the opportunities in this life to turn back to Him when we stumble, and this is His basis for separating the sheep from the goats (Matthew 25:32-33).

Buddhism and Christianity both seek detachment from things in nature, and acknowledge the existence of suffering in this world, but for contrasting reasons.

Buddhism speaks of escaping suffering by getting past impermanent, desirable creation. This involves denying the soul's reality or permanence altogether.

Christianity, on the other hand, recognizes that all desires are to be satisfied only in God. Sin is the inability to fully desire according to God's will. A soul, loved by God, doesn't shun suffering, but rather sees in it his salvation, as exemplified by Christ the incarnate God on the cross.

This chapter is not meant as an extensive description of varying doctrines, suffice to say that differences in doctrine do matter in how we accept truth when it appears in our lives.

Even as we acknowledge how false doctrine could mislead us into acting contrary to His commandments, it's a humbling thought that even among those of other faiths, are saintly beings upon whom He looks with favor. To be sure, we're all children of the one true God, capable of showing His goodness and love in our lives. Since He is truth, it isn't too far out to suppose or hope that He is capable of manifesting among those still ignorant of the Word "through no fault of their own," as the Vatican II dogmatic constitution *Lumen gentium* phrases it. We need not doubt stories of non-Christian monks and contemplatives who exude love in every gesture and have great things to say about compassion and peace.

This doesn't make other religions equally valid. Adherents of other faiths, which may have a spark here and there of truth, would have to achieve holiness in spite of the doctrinal errors they are exposed to.

Knowing of good people from other religions shouldn't stop one's pursuit of the Church in which He has continually provided His grace through the centuries. Non-Catholic followers of Christ do develop a personal relationship with Him wherein their faith is evident in their works, but this doesn't make it any less lamentable that they're missing out on receiving Jesus in the Eucharist, a privilege unappreciated even by most Catholics. Similarly, people we admire who still don't know Jesus as the only Son of God ought to be told so, for their benefit as much as their followers'.

If you browse through the Religion/Spirituality section of a bookstore or library, you'll notice how a lot of pagan writings love to take Jesus' name in vain, allying Him with whatever belief system they propose in place of Catholic, Apostolic* Christianity.

* That which is passed on by the Christ-appointed Apostles themselves.

Leo Tolstoy, unsatisfied with what he saw as the superstitious chatter in the Gospel, fashioned his own 'gospel,' called 'The Gospel in brief,' reducing Jesus to a reciter of wise sayings, the Resurrection itself considered "superfluous." To Tolstoy, this was "truth," to be saved from the "perverted" meaning Christians had given Jesus' teachings.

Yogi Paramahansa Yogananda, a forerunner of the New Age movement, loved to interpret Scripture in light of Hindu doctrine, providing an alternative meaning to these writings whose message he felt was lost on most people such as the Church hierarchy. His autobiography expresses admiration for Jesus reserved only for other spiritual masters close to his heart. He even narrates having an ecstatic vision of Christ Himself, taker of the world's karma.

New Age author Caroline Myss tries to pass off the writings of Catholic mystic Saint Teresa of Avila as a nondenominational look at the soul's journey before achieving the unity of the "trinity" of cosmic forces: matter, the soul, and enlightened consciousness. Gone is the person of Jesus, actually the three Persons of the Holy Trinity, in favor of impersonal symbols that encompass existence.

Christian authors, on the other hand, don't attempt parallels between the Bible and pagan figures, or claim that all religions spring from the same source, just to reel in non-practicing Christians and non-Christians. You should hold suspect anything that detracts from the loving sacrifice Jesus made. Christ *is* truth. He'll have none of that.

Are we really to believe that God only revealed His word in one place on Earth, while leaving the rest in darkness?

That's what evangelizing is for! It's an ongoing process. Spreading God's word is not just to bug your relatives and friends once in a while, but to reach people from different cultures who haven't been as fortunate as us yet. You just don't know what effect you could have on those you get to connect with from areas where churches are few and far between. Keep asking Jesus to use you. You may be wondering what the odds are that He hasn't revealed Himself yet to another, not realizing that it is precisely through you that He intends to reveal Himself.

When you know Jesus is in your life, you'll know He ought to be in everyone's life. Even those whom you dismiss as too far to reach. We're all called to spread the Gospel, and that means, to the whole world. Let's not exclude nonbelievers, like the Gentiles were excluded during the pre-Christian era. Jesus is for all, and the more you recognize His hand in your life, the more you'll sense an obligation to share His truth.

Imagine receiving free cake at your doorstep. You don't know where it's from, but you try the cake anyway, and it's delicious. And this repeats itself every morning. You get to enjoy the cake, but are you going to just leave it like that? Wouldn't you want to know from whom this delightful treat is coming? That's kind of like what Jesus' love is like, minus the bloatedness. We often are unable to acknowledge the ways He blesses us and others of different faiths, who do show Christ-like qualities but may not know the significance of His name. He gives us His blessings anyway, inviting all of us to know Him. All we need to do is ask.

Evangelizing is not about getting others to live 'a good life' *per se*, of getting people to be kind to one another, but letting them know where this kindness comes from. Evangelizing is about knowing God our Creator as a person who loves us completely. How many relationships do you have where you don't know the other one's name? There comes a point, however awkward, where you have to ask, "Oh, by the way, what's your name? Funny how it never came up before."

In a sense, we all start off not knowing Christianity, even when we go through lower and secondary education in a Christian school. Each one's life situation is a starting point for Jesus to work His way in. However seemingly near or far we are, grace bridges the gaps.

Is the Christmas holiday just a pagan rip-off used in the late Roman Empire to pander to non-Christians? A loud majority thinks so, while others point to documents written before Rome's acceptance of Christianity in the 4th century, that refer to Jesus' birth on December 25 or His conception nine months prior on March 25.

My personal opinion is that God, that is, Jesus of the Bible, willed that we would celebrate His birth during a specific time of the year. And future archaeology and scholarship will find that He was indeed born during winter time. You don't have to subscribe to this. Anyway, none of this changes the fact that the Christmas holiday was set as God willed it, and serves to commemorate the very real incarnation of He who saves us from death.

6. 'Conscience is just fear of being caught'

If human action is nothing but reward and punishment, I suppose conscience could be reduced to a matter of fear. But when you acknowledge the more encompassing reality of a God that is constantly revealing Himself to you, then conscience becomes a way for you to know your standing with Him.

If conscience is a matter of avoiding being caught, what's to bring convicts on death row to repentance, as occasionally happens? A belief that they'll somehow escape prison before being executed, only to be caught again? Or perhaps these convicts mistakenly turn on this adaptive feature when all hope is lost, and we're left to think, "That poor idiot. He's already condemned to die, and He's *still* sorry for committing his crime!"

This might also make for the allegation that the most virtuous of people are the most scared. I don't mean the fear of God, which should be our response the more aware we are of His greatness and mercy, but scared like terrified, anxious, and paranoid. I suppose saints are sticklers for perfection and are more ardent in their repentance, but such exacting consciences are yet distinct from the clinical neuroticism skeptics would like to accuse them of.

'Conscience is just fear of being caught'

Are we then to explain the peace of mind of the obedient as the ability to sublimate one's fears into smug certainty, once they know they're in the good graces of their imagined supreme being? This is a little bit nearer to the truth at least. Conscience isn't determined by our relationship with society, but by our relationship with God, however much we recognize Him for Who He is. Even if you were the only one left alive on Earth after a nuclear explosion, or were stranded on an island with no hope of return to a human community, God will still be there letting you know how you're doing.

If you don't nurture your relationship with Him, your ability to tell what's wrong and what's right suffers. With faith, you know of the love that He has for you and that He's shown you as both God and man, by which you pray to Him all the more sincerely, and trust in His will, rather than in your abilities.

In conversion stories I hear, C.S. Lewis' 'Mere Christianity' comes up rather often, in which former atheists recount being swayed from their unbelief by Lewis' arguments and flair. I can't say the same when my mother gave me a copy of the book for Christmas 2007. Even my appreciation of Lewis' Narnia books did not keep me from feeling offended at his Jesus talk, all of which I took to be fantasy world building.

Here are some choice cringey comments I made on the book that reveal my hard-hearted intellectual pride at the time:

"Indeed, *mere* Christianity."

"Just because I refuse to personify that so-called God does not mean I refuse human virtues."

"Clive ['C.S.' stands for 'Clive Staples'] is a real idiot. He uses the word nonsense about other ideas contrary to his own, and he places these nonsense ideas next to nonsense ideas of his own."

"The entire bible [I had lowercased it intentionally], including 'historical' facts such as Jesus' birth, is literary, not literal. It's myth, whose noncultural aspects are that which remain timeless."

"Stick to the facts, Staples."

There's a lot more, and a lot worse. I'm so embarrassed now at my righteous indignation that Lewis would invoke God and universal morality, in contrast to my perspective of limiting reality to physical material, anything beyond of which could only be acceptable in a figurative sense. Morals weren't determined by God, but were a human calculation of pros and cons, for the sake of peace of mind. All one had to do to be good was to not trample on another's rights, and this was what made for social harmony, which is all anybody could expect.

When studying politics and law without God as foundation, there's a danger of narrowing the scope of morals to the strictly legal, outside of which one's actions and interior life are deemed nobody's business. Aside from consideration of one's 'rational self-interest,' nothing is to limit one's free expression in words and actions.

Humanism may not sound all that bad, but it conceals a mind poisoned by skepticism. A love for some abstract 'humanity' might be claimed, but there is little love left for people.

What a change it's been! The difference between my fake nobility back then and my not-being-as-much-of-a-jerk today, is, quite simply, faith.

7. A world of suffering

> *Look into the eyes of a newborn baby, and tell me they have original sin! Your guilt-tripping is what poisons their innocence!*

Jesus Himself tells us that it is to those like children that the Kingdom of Heaven belongs (Matthew 19:14). But this doesn't mean we could sidestep the dogma of original sin. If a child was free of original sin, like Mother Mary, then all the evil influences of the world would not tarnish their innocence as they grow older.

However you interpret the literalness of Adam and Eve's sinfulness being passed down to us, doesn't change the reality of sin and the corresponding hardships in which we live. To claim that we're simply corrupted by the world but otherwise pure just begs the question of why such corruption exists in the first place. To dismiss the very idea of sin does nothing to eliminate its manifestations, in particular, physical suffering and death.

Nonbelievers try to find consolation in saying, "Death is a natural part of life. It's what gives meaning to it all." In the absence of faith, it sounds practical, because what else could you do when doomed to mortality? But I don't buy the 'it's natural' argument, which could also be used to justify all sorts of bodily indulgence and the disease that 'naturally' follows. The good news is that in Jesus we have reason to aspire to more than a few decades of earthly toil.

One common reading of the Book of Job is that God tries to prove to the devil that Job would never give up his faith, and so allows the devil to unleash terrible things on the man. In the end, it is Job's blind faith that gets him back on God's good side. Interpreted this way, Job's suffering is ultimately meaningless, part of a sick game for God's amusement.

This faithless view doesn't distinguish between blind, mindless belief, and trust in all He does. What's missing in the above narrative is that God only allows such evils to happen for the growth of our souls, *if* we maintain our trust in Him. Saint Faustina was assured by her guardian angel that whatever encounters she would have with evil spirits were only with Jesus' permission, and that was enough for her to accept His will. It is with similar trust that Job accepted his lack of understanding of the whys of his situation, knowing that God is always in charge (Job 42:2-3).

The Lord values the trust we have in Him, however emotionally rewarding this is in facing tribulation in the world.

It is in the question of suffering that our pride often surfaces, that we know better about running worlds. Yet the Bible dismisses presumptions of knowledge almost from the get-go, in Genesis 3:4-6, with smart satan deceiving Eve into thinking that eating the forbidden fruit would make her and Adam wise, godlike. The attractiveness of the fruit itself was the devil's deceit. From there come the hazy justifications for what sins we allow ourselves to indulge in.

I heard rock musician Geddy Lee say in an interview that it was his parents' experience in Nazi concentration camps that convinced him that there is no God. Yet unbelief was not the only response of those who experienced the horrors of the Holocaust. Saints Maximilian Kolbe and Edith Stein had their opportunities to flee from their occupied countries, but strong in their faith, chose instead to join the Jewish people to their deaths. Kolbe asked to take the place of a fellow prisoner who had been picked to die by starvation, and Stein, even before her capture, offered her life to the Lord so that her fellow Jews may be converted.

Christians hold a faith that more important than even life or death is union with Him, to undo our brokenness. We invite Him into our lives, in spite of our reservations based on our limited understanding of how things 'should be.' Faith isn't so much about shutting up, but about opening ourselves to the truth that is Jesus, and because He is true, we get to find out for ourselves how little our objections mean in His presence.

8. Jesus' unfair death

Doing good shouldn't be a matter of guilt-tripping, but of wanting to live a good life, right? On the face of it, Jesus' Passion seems to be a matter of placing blame on us, for what was done by His murderers 2,000 years ago. Where's the justice in that? Moreover, shouldn't we be guided by compassion for those around us, recognizing their dignity, in treating them with respect and helping them? Why should the suffering of a man, even if this man is God, motivate us to do good?

Whether or not we acknowledge Jesus as God, we do want to be kind to others. That in itself should compel us to the good, leaving aside that all goodness does come from God Himself. Once we acknowledge Jesus as God, however, we also know that what we do to others is done to Him. He suffers not just for the sins we directly commit against others, but also in the things that we think of in private.

We go to the Eucharist and pray the Divine Mercy Chaplet on the assumption that Jesus Christ the Son is offered as a sacrifice to the Father, in place of anything we could offer, none of which gives us life. It's not just difficult but impossible to wrap our head around this mystery, let alone see how this could be fair to God, who both died for our sins and gave His most beloved Son to die for our sins. But a refusal to accept His sacrifice earns us the rebuke of Jesus Himself who says, "Get behind me, Satan!" (Matthew 16:23).

In a merely human sense, it's completely unfair that God died for our sins, but it is in accepting such 'unfair' terms as laid out by Jesus that we glimpse His mercy and love, that we know that according to His will, He gives each of us more than enough opportunity to accept Him and eternal life.

Such 'unfairness' also allows us to more confidently submit to whatever we have and whatever happens to us in life, including not being graced in the same way as the saints are. However unfair we perceive our situation, the corresponding 'unfairness' of God the Father providing His Son as an offering to save us from all evil more than makes up for it. If only we accept the unfolding of our lives and His sacrifice, as His will.

BECAUSE SCIENCE
(whatever that means)

9. BEAN

This chapter, and the succeeding chapters tackling science and reason, could be summed up by saying that *science and nature have been deified in place of God.*

BEAN is an observation of mine, of the fourfold approach by which science lulls us into indifference to God. It stands for:
Big Bang
Evolution
Archetypes
Neurons

The Big Bang and Evolution are cited as true stories of creation unlike that one in Genesis with an apple in it. It is reasoned that if the physical universe did start as a super dense mass that eventually expanded to what we know as galaxies and stars and planets, and if the form which we humans take is a result of gradual changes over many generations, what need do we have for the Lord and His six days and Adam and Eve?

Meanwhile, archetypes dismiss the divine as mere symbols that illustrate the human condition. If other cultures tell us of a great mother figure, then Mother Mary must be one such figure, a mere myth.

And neurons. There's something about studying the nervous system, observing the electrochemical processes in the brain, that makes some scientists presume they know everything there is to know about everything.

It takes a while in consideration of each letter of the BEAN to say, wait a minute, this doesn't explain *anything*! Nor does it really try to. We're so caught up in our materialism that we limit ourselves to descriptions of observable phenomena with whatever technology is in vogue, and proudly state, "Because science."

Science's insufficiency is not just a matter of quantity of knowledge, but the *kind* of knowledge. None of BEAN explains or *could* explain our 'hereness.' Taking any of them as evidence of God's absence misleads us into thinking we've got the answers when all that materialism gives us are yet other things to ask, such as:

What was there before the Big Bang?

Why did we evolve *this* way?

Why is *this* archetype so prominent?

What is it that manifests itself in the very particular ways our brains work?

Even stating that we are made in God's image has more explaining power, e.g. Because that's how He made us. The difference between invoking God and invoking impersonal processes in nature is that in the former, the inquirer is invited to know the truth in a personal manner. Nature on its own only invites more questions backwards into time.

Explaining religion as some defense mechanism or evolutionary safeguard requiring self-deceit isn't more 'realistic' than a position of faith. Such a materialistic interpretation speaks in cold, 'objective' terms in an attempt to deny meaning to life, in stark contrast to the ultimate significance found in a relationship with God, something we get to know not through abstractions, but direct experience.

Adaptation as an explanation for the eternal joy in contemplation of God, only makes sense if we weren't there to say otherwise. But we are. The world isn't merely observed, it's lived in. God had to have made it so. And if God could make it so, it's not too far out to think He might seek to reach out to those He created, out of what we might initially surmise to be love, only later discovering that indeed He *is* love. And making Himself known is what someone who loves us would do.

Dismissing Jesus' appearance to saints and His manifestation in various ways as biological mechanisms, just begs the question of what's driving such a mechanism. This perpetual question begging is not going to stop. Skeptics might end up claiming no ultimate answers could be found, while the fullness of truth is clear to the faithful. How do we resolve the impasse?

Faith is borne of knowing our being here is of something rather than of nothing. It takes an education in jargon and depersonalized 'objectifying' of our experiences to deny the reality of our living here and now.

Related to BEAN is the idea of aliens. The indefiniteness of speculations of what advanced species could be, serves to deny any truth in what we in our relatively primitive technology have yet discovered. No way can we be made in God's image. Our future evolved species and extraterrestrials are way more wondrous than we can imagine! Or so we imagine, in our inability to get past our extreme skepticism.

However advanced civilization gets, the Word remains. Being a human person will never be irrelevant, however crazy your predictions of the future are. Jesus the man is still the one to be known.

Related to evolution is the idea that religion itself, especially when it looks down on 'the world'*, is a mere neurosis adopted by humans who in their weakness seek power by denigrating nature. This idea as perpetuated by the likes of Friedrich Nietzsche and Alfred Adler once appealed to me, but only upon my conversion or reversion did I see how *small* a viewpoint this *will to diagnose* was, in comparison to my life that has in fact been enriched and empowered since saying "Yes, of course" to Jesus.

* 'The world,' as referred to in the Bible, does not refer to creation in itself, which God saw as "very good" (Genesis 1:31) but rather to a specific, narrowed interpretation of creation as disconnected from its Creator.

For all the talk of science and reason, materialists make one large unfounded assumption about nature that guides their invocation of BEAN: that things happen randomly. An evolutionist may talk about some underlying survival principle behind a species' mutations, but still claim a randomness in the occurrence of such mutations.

Our faith, however, looks at all things and events as having their purpose. There is nothing that God doesn't will specifically for His glory.

Who's right then? You might say it's a matter of believing or not believing. However, I would maintain that the burden of proof is on those who assume randomness, for they have to negate the causality by which any meaningful scientific statements are made, e.g. heat causes objects to expand. Those of the faith who attribute purposefulness to the events of their lives at least use cause and effect consistently, e.g. God is the cause of everything.

It's more logical to believe something happened for a reason than that it "just happened." How could it have happened then? How much of 'the butterfly effect,' the 'uncertainty principle,' and 'dark matter' is really just experts tossing their hands up in frustration, in their inability to account for cause and effect in their observations?

Accepting your ignorance is the first step in acknowledging the truth of a Creator, even when you still hesitate to assume the characteristics of such a being.

Admittedly it's one thing to believe things have their causes, and another thing to believe that there is a divine will behind every single aspect of our daily lives. But maybe you could better see how purpose is not just wishful thinking, and is more consistent with the causality of creation.

We are here for a reason, and this is evident if you acknowledge that you are one who experiences. Creation is meant to be lived in, and you know this because you're living in it. It's not neurons or biological chemicals that experience events. Trying to detach yourself like that is simply willful blindness.

Even if you see how BEAN is unable to explain God away, you might take the stance, as I did for a long time, that the ultimate meaning to life is a mystery, and will stay a mystery. Whether this means a life after death or not, shouldn't get in the way of living a life of prudence and consideration of others. Which is all any divine being could ask of us, right?

This agnostic view rightly downplays the intellectual insufficiency of BEAN materialism, but also washes its hands of knowing anything for certain. But taking this shoulder-shrugging position itself assumes that a Creator is impersonal. Without meaning to, the agnostic gets intimidated by all the light years and eons and 'randomness' of things into saying, "Okay whatever God is, I don't know. I don't even care to know!" revealing a no less atheistic stance after all.

Agnosticism allows us to be in awe of our awareness of being here, but stops short of attributing anything to our Creator. Which is another assumption, of the Creator going through the trouble of creating conscious beings but being too much of a tease to reveal anything in common with us, something by which we could have a relationship with it.

My faith lies in the not too unreasonable supposition that our Creator intentionally reveals *Himself* in a very specific institution in history, through which He has revealed His word in a very specific book, the understanding of which is guided by this same institution.

10. Energy

We're so used to talking about our activities in terms of energy. We say that we just don't have the energy to exercise, or that this guy we heard on TV was a high-energy guy, and the like. Soon enough, we start to view not just the natural world as a matter (no pun intended) of energy distribution, but our moral lives themselves seem determined by natural processes we seek control over, like 'The Force' in 'Star wars.'

Indeed, much of Oriental philosophies speak of the harnessing of energies, and their flow through energy centers. This scientized view of human volition has its proponents, who swear by the benefits of Yoga and Tai Chi, equating these to spiritual goodness. Even relationships become an "exchange of energy" where we have to keep from being infected by others' bad moods by channeling such negativity through proper breathing and keeping that spine straight.

However, the upkeep of our souls could not be limited to technique. Our relationship with God is more dynamic than what visualizations we manage to conjure up. We have free will, and our lives are enriched by God's grace, in ways that aren't reflected primarily in biological or physical terms. When we limit our idea of the divine to be a kind of science, in the sense of impersonal processes of regularity, spirituality is reduced to a positioning of power, where the weakest are also the least 'evolved,' whose concerns could be done away with.

The more you turn away from religion, the more 'scientific' religion seems like a good idea. Doing good becomes a matter of systematic action rather than a following of conscience and God's inspired Word. One's pursuit of holiness is replaced with a vision of universal evolution, with love and goodness being just other words for rapturous efficiency.

11. 'In this day and age'

I remember once watching 'You don't know Jack' (2010) and being inspired by the advocacy for euthanasia. As the movie shows, the issue's complicated. Which more than often means, it's a hard decision, but should be considered a 'choice' anyway. In the movie, the pro-life position is depicted as primitive and insensitive to the individual cases in which 'mercy' killing is considered. Dr. Jack Kevorkian rails against these remnants of obsolete religion, lamenting how in this day and age, people still can't ask to be killed!

The life of a suffering person could only be seen as expendable when we don't recognize Jesus suffering with them every step of the way. But I'd like to focus on the implication that we modern people are somehow more civilized, compassionate, and moral than people who believe in things that defy our limited scientific understanding. This includes a lot of crazies even today, e.g. religious folk.

The impression of a morally superior present is at least partially based on advances in technology, where one's actions both in public and in private could be better monitored to ensure compliance with the law.

We assume all people were vulgar and ruthless in the time before science saved us all. But many today are just as vulgar and ruthless as those we decry from years past. The difference is we get to be vulgar and ruthless using our cars (road rage), the internet (flame wars), and other innovations. And we find it harder and harder to believe that Jesus Christ, a Jew from 2,000 years ago, is God who suffered on the cross for sins we commit *today*.

I suspect that the arrogance of 'in this day and age' is an offshoot of the 19th-century evolution craze, where the observation of natural selection in a species over time has been taken as proof that God has nothing to do with our being here and alive. We conclude that now is *certainly* and *inevitably* better. It just has to be. Even our physiologies and neurologies, in comparison to the brutes of yesteryear, reflect more peaceful dispositions. Goodness is a matter of impersonal processes in our brains.

If you don't believe the Bible is God's inspired word in the first place, or that it contains the truth (John 14:6), then it's easy to dismiss its relevance to today's hot issues, and not so hot issues, such as how you think of your neighbor. It becomes easy to assume that we could determine by sheer reason what is good and what is bad (Genesis 3:5), and that we should fashion nature, and ourselves, as *we* know to be right. Where to go from this *evolved* way of thinking, but away from God?

CATHOLIFE

12. Brothers and sisters in Christ

We all know we're not supposed to believe in love as depicted in movies. Not even the 'realistic' award winners that casualize divorce and its related phenomena, sleeping over and living in. Yet we can't help but be influenced by what we're exposed to day in and day out.

Our knowledge of love could only be degraded, anytime we step away from the Bible and allow ourselves to be guided by Hollywood.

The accusation is that the Church is full of closed-minded bishops and priests who think that sex is dirty. Why wouldn't they 'do it' otherwise?

On the contrary, it's our 'modern,' worldly view of sex that doesn't fully appreciate the preciousness of our bodies as given by God.

What do we know of love from the Bible? We know it was why God the Father sent His only Son to us (John 3:16), that there is no greater love than the laying down of one's life for one's friends (John 15:13), and that love is patient and kind, and never boastful, among other beautiful attributes (1 Corinthians 13:4). Most would readily agree with these, but Jesus expounds on what such love entails in human affairs. In Matthew 5 and 19, not only is divorce denied, but Jesus expands the idea of adultery to include even looking at someone with lust. And to explain such stringent standards, He harks back to the Book of Genesis.

In the beginning, we find Adam beholding Eve for the first time and declaring her "bone of my bones and flesh of my flesh" (Genesis 2:23). In their nakedness, they "were not ashamed" (Genesis 2:25). It is only with the fall of Man (Genesis 3) that their view of one another becomes 'adulterated,' and they conceal their nakedness from one another, and God. Reading these verses through modern eyes, they sound like an excuse to engage in 'free love,' with the innocent promiscuity of animals. Except we're not just animals in God's eyes. What we are made more aware of through the Genesis story is the strife caused by engaging in behaviors that deviate from what our Lord intended. It's not sexuality to be rejected, but the notion that it could have a significance in our lives apart from God's plan, of allowing us to participate in the creation of life.

Contrary to most love songs, the Bible doesn't speak of love and marriage in terms of how great they feel. In the book of Tobit, Tobit's son Tobias expresses a similar notion of chastity as what we saw "in the beginning," when speaking of his new wife Sarah: "I am not taking this sister of mine because of lust, but with sincerity" (Tobit 8:7)*. Another translation reads, "... but for a noble purpose" (New American Bible). The virtue is evidently not in the pleasure, but in the service. He calls her a sister, at least in the RSV translation of the Bible; such is his purity.

* Those of you who've read Saint Pope John Paul II's 'Theology of the body' see quite plainly that I'm riffing off of it in elaborating on the Matthew, Genesis, and Tobit verses.

In Genesis 29, Jacob works seven years in Laban's house in order to take Laban's daughter Rachel as his wife. We're told that the time passes like days for Jacob, in his love for Rachel. However, when Rachel's sister Leah is dumped on him instead, he finds out he has to serve Laban another seven years, or a total of 14 years, for Rachel's hand in marriage, which Jacob manages. The story is pretty bizarre, but is a remarkable illustration of steadfastness even when unforeseen setbacks occur and fruits of consolation are scarce.

In the Gospel, Jesus, even when affirming his command over the Apostles, says, "But I am among you as one who serves" (Luke 22:27). "If I then, your Lord and Teacher, have washed your feet, you also ought to wash one another's feet." (John 13:14).

The 1968 encyclical *Humanae Vitae* states two purposes of the conjugal act between husband and wife: that of unity, and that of procreation. Furthermore, these purposes could not be separated from one another.

Such a teaching is now considered old-fashioned and unrealistic. It sounds like conservative finger wagging meant to keep people from living their lives the way they think best. The prevailing attitude is that as long as it's voluntary, it doesn't hurt anybody.

However, there are those who, like priests and nuns, choose one of the Church's prescriptions, of celibacy, and are enriched for it. Jesus Himself makes a special association between voluntary celibacy and the Kingdom of Heaven (Matthew 19:12). It may be a cross to bear, with its own struggles and temptations, but these are present whatever lifestyle one chooses, including marriage.

It is in shifting our focus away from worldly enticements that chastity, celibacy, and the dreaded virginity are most instructive.

13. Make virginity cool again

The point of view below is not something that guided me throughout my life, but only upon getting more immersed in the doctrine. Like most baptized Catholics, I did not give the Church the last say on things, and I felt free to consider what the Catechism said on some or many issues as outdated and even unhealthy. Sex as strictly a marital act just seemed a little excessive, if the worry was unwanted pregnancy or disease.

As if it is only *minimization of consequences* that we have to concern ourselves with in determining right and wrong. I suppose education in Catholicism could step up a little more, but when you consider the media monster we're up against, it almost seems preferable to let boys be boys, and girls, be girls. But that's exactly what gets us into trouble.

Even my favorite shows mock the 'undersexed.' One character has had only x number of partners in their life. Another hasn't had sex in y number of years. Or a character's virginity becomes the springboard for some wacky, zany adventure.

Make virginity cool again

Then we have 'The 40 year old virgin' (2005) and its assumption of the terrible humiliation of 'not getting some' for a whopping four decades. We're made to believe that the only way one could be a virgin that age is not for lack of trying. Virginity couldn't possibly be a choice. The movie's saving grace though is that the hero's fear, of the leading lady not loving him as a virgin, proves unfounded.

Culture is so twisted that being a virgin is most often equated to being a loser. You'll find such mockery among Christians, even though the greatest man Who ever lived on Earth, Jesus Himself, is a virgin. The greatest woman who ever lived on Earth, Mother Mary, is a virgin. From this alone, we could see how Hollywoodized our understanding has become.

I don't know anything and don't care squat about the NFL but Tim Tebow is a hero of mine. He's outspokenly religious and pro-life in an increasingly secularized world, and it's extra cool to know that he spent his first few years in Manila, where I live. And up until his recent marriage, he wore his virginity proudly. It's such an unusual advocacy for an American football player to have. Contrast that with basketball legend Wilt Chamberlain's 20,000-women 'statistic.'

Admittedly, an unchaste virgin could be as sinful as some wanton fornicator. It's still chastity that counts. But as with any relationship, if you're not bringing each other to holiness, you have no business with each other.

There's the argument of 'repression' of one's drives, which supposedly will inevitably explode in an even more depraved manner unless there was some outlet of release. But that's a sad excuse for not altering one's erroneous view of sex as primarily a means of pleasure. Which goes back to the purposes of the conjugal act as discussed in *Humanae Vitae*, of unity between husband and wife, and procreativity.

But what about the technological means to divide these two purposes, namely contraception? I'd liken it to gift wrapping, without the gift inside. When we act with half-hearted intention, without the openness to creating life, we have nothing to give another but an empty package. This should guide us when we think of going about it 'for fun' or 'for experience,' or of giving in out of wedlock when 'it's real love anyway.'

We have to be especially cautious about losing our faith on account of what couldn't be dismissed as merely raging hormones. Lust is an all-too-easy way the devil turns people away from the Lord.

Our judgments apart from God are faulty, our feelings deceitful. If we don't consult God in everything, if we decide what it is that God says rather than what we could trust to be His very word, then our actions will keep us broken. If we remember that God really is here with us as we contemplate engaging in sin, we could better overcome worldly desires, and resist the appeal of the 'shiny and new.'

14. Mother Mary

If you're going to get closer to Jesus, you also have to develop your relationship with those who knew and loved Him best: Mother Mary and Saint Joseph. Later in His life on Earth, it was His Apostles, particularly Peter and John, whom Jesus associated with the most, but it's a completely different thing to actually have been the ones to wash and feed Him, to teach Him how to speak. And all this responsibility while knowing He was God. Their finding of the 12-year-old Jesus in the Jerusalem temple is the only incident of His youth recorded in the Gospel, but already hints at the roller-coaster they went through; "and His mother kept all these things in her heart" (Luke 2:51).

In here we see that Mother Mary, though without sin, isn't omniscient. She isn't God. She's still sinless, but wouldn't know where to find Jesus when He goes missing, unless the Lord lets her know. She was reminded by Jesus of the Father's primacy in her son's activities.

I didn't know this when I first seriously got into Catholicism, but we're supposed to believe that even after Christ's birth, Mother Mary stayed a virgin. It was like Jesus was raised by a nun and a priest, which actually sounds quite practical when you're entrusted with the holiest of missions.

Whatever holiness allowed her, of all women, to give birth to our Savior, was tied to a lifelong commitment to celibacy, I now see. This isn't an indictment against our procreative powers, which the Book of Genesis reveals are a gift from God, but a recognition of the special role she would play in the Church's history. When women become nuns, they vow to stay celibate; it's really not much harder to believe that she made a similar vow as a young woman.

What may be even harder to believe is that Saint Joseph would put up with such an arrangement. But that he would likewise be committed to celibacy does show how wise God was in appointing Saint Joseph as Jesus' foster father and spouse of the Blessed Virgin. Denying himself normal husbandly rights was itself a show of love towards his wife and son, like how a priest's foregoing of marriage and children allows him to serve his parish more single-mindedly. This man was found worthy by the Father to be the lord of Jesus' household. I somehow doubt that staying celibate was Saint Joseph's biggest challenge in the years of being responsible for the upbringing of the Son of God Himself.

Mother Mary is the clearest of lenses through which the light that is Jesus passes through unfiltered, undistorted. Which is probably why the words used in veneration of her, sound like blasphemy to Protestants, but if one knows that Mary's fullness of grace comes solely from God the Creator and not her a mere creation, it's much easier to give her her due.

We can pray for her intercession, as to any saint, for her prayers are especially powerful. Oftentimes, your prayers might be spoken almost in shorthand, as though you were asking *her* to grant this or that, even though you know it is through the Holy Spirit that *her* prayers have effect. Put this way, you shouldn't have qualms petitioning her.

If Mother Mary ever appears to me in person, there is really only one thing I could tell her: the 'Hail Mary.' I can't imagine ever having a set of talking points or questions that are of greater spiritual benefit, than what this brief prayer contains. And if I do the Rosary while seeing her before my very eyes, I will still recite the other Rosary prayers, such as the 'Our Father' and 'Glory Be.' She loves me and everyone I love; she will wait her turn.

The 'Hail Mary' seems straightforward, of acknowledging that she is full of grace and blessed, in connection with being Jesus' mother, for which you could ask her to pray for you. But you are also acknowledging *her* mercy, as two other prayers, the 'Memorare' ("Despise not my petitions but in your mercy, hear and answer me") and 'Hail Holy Queen' ("Mother of Mercy") state more explicitly.

The sins you commit don't only hurt Jesus. A sword pierces Mary's heart as well (Luke 2:35). This is especially clear when praying the five Sorrowful Mysteries of the Rosary in which Jesus' Passion is traced, from the Agony in the Garden, to the Scourging at the Pillar, to the Crowning with Thorns, to the Carrying of the Cross, and to the Crucifixion. With this in mind, we could ask this most blessed woman for her prayers, in spite of our sinfulness, with greater humility and gratitude.

15. Demon wrestling

Anyone born with original sin is not *fully* qualified to be talking about fighting temptation. Even saints won't always hit the mark, although you have to take note that their moral standards are much higher than ours. I'm fairly new in this pursuit to be holy, but hope that my words will be of use to you anyway.

The hardest sins to avoid are the ones not prepared for, the ones in which to some degree you knowingly place yourself in temptation. This may be a matter of going to places where such sins are known to take place, or of simply letting your thoughts fester unabated until *pow* someone gets hurt, whether with your words, your fists, or even your eyes.

Prayer could be an effective deterrent in that you reorient yourself away from the all-natural tendency to succumb. And if you don't feel Jesus, Mother Mary, or the saints are with you, that's part of the temptation as well. Take that as your cue to pray even harder.

If you keep Christ in your thoughts every time, knowing He's there for you in your temptation, and if you talk to Him through your temptation, telling Him what's in your heart that you can't seem to help but turn to sin, the less temptation will hold you.

Temptation never truly goes away on Earth, but that doesn't mean you can't always ask Jesus for another turn, which He in His merciful love grants. You have to believe in His mercy most of all, an eternal mercy.

16. Entertainment

I'm less entertained nowadays. And I know that makes me sound like a snob, like someone who boasts they're too good to have a TV at home. What happened to me is probably similar to how old folks grumble that the movies, shows, and music were better in the old days (they were). Except even my former favorites leave me indifferent after several minutes.

This was such a change for me. As a fan, I'd watch TV episodes again and again, and would understand inside jokes among internet communities. I'd make notes on the various connections between episodes, and themes or topics explored, and complain mostly to myself about errors in continuity. It was pretty dorky.

I also got into movies in a big way. I may not have been a complete buff, but I'd watch a couple of the Oscar nominees in a given year, and would take note of when my next rewatching of, say, 'The godfather' or 'Star wars' was due, which was something like every couple of years. I was fairly informed, enthusiastic, and most importantly, opinionated.

The more engrossed you get in the most important thing, being with Jesus, you see more clearly how other things don't have a point in themselves. And moving away from these former joys is not something done on purpose, but rather merely observed.

You might find it better to cut down on these shows anyway. Watching even PG-13 scenes *could be* troublesome in trying to build a prayer life. But at least you can be confident that you're not missing much by looking away, or shutting off the TV altogether.

Before I fully embraced my Catholicism, I remember getting similar advice of giving up such entertainment, and I thought of how being too wary about kissing scenes or gruesome murders on TV was giving TV way too much power over one's state of mind. We don't want to become so easily stimulated or oversensitive either, right? But now that I myself have become a square, I could see how there really is no point in filling one's head with these things, even if there is a good story behind them.

You don't have to make a list of pros and cons of all your recreational habits, but the more intent you are in praying, the more naturally you move away from what you've got to admit is often mindless, even depraved, entertainment. *Tama na iyan.* Enough of that.

When you see that your mission in life, everyone's really, is to let others know of Jesus' love, everything else is put into perspective. Not to say we should no longer participate in 'fun,' particularly activities of a social nature, but these are to be used as

Entertainment

platforms for His glory. Like Stephen Curry stepping onto the basketball court with his Philippians 4:13 tattoo ("I can do all things in Him who strengthens me") for all the world to see.

17. Politics

A lot of our perception of politics is swayed by superficial media, and the more time we take to contemplate God, the more the scales on our eyes fall off, and we recognize His hand even in current events, by which we form our positions on a variety of topics. Who's in power is not as important as knowing that God willed their being in power for a reason. And the more we hate them, the better for us to pray for them.

I'm not trying to tell you what ideology to embrace, suffice to say that whatever 'system' there is, it must place mercy over justice. As Portia in William Shakespeare's 'The merchant of Venice' said on mercy:

> 'Tis mightiest in the mightiest; it becomes
> The thronèd monarch better than his crown.
> His scepter shows the force of temporal power,
> The attribute to awe and majesty
> Wherein doth sit the dread and fear of kings;
> But mercy is above this sceptered sway.
> It is enthronèd in the hearts of kings;
> It is an attribute to God Himself...

Portia's monologue hints at barely a fraction of God's ocean of mercy.

'Mercy over justice' (MOJ) risks being understood as a rationale for disregarding economic realities* in carrying out one's social advocacies. Thus we must emphasize the morality of the manner by which police forces implement such policies.

* We have to distinguish between awareness of economic principles, and using cost-benefit analysis as an excuse to criticize another's sincere offering, as Judas did to Mary sister of Martha when she anointed Jesus with an expensive ointment at Bethany (John 12:1-8).

MOJ also risks being gamed by evil psychopaths feigning penitence. Thus informed public opinion must have its influence in holding suspects accountable.

Jesus asks us to render to Caesar what is Caesar's, and to God what is God's (Matthew 22:21). I take this to mean that we can grumble and complain all we want, but whatever obligations to the state we could not escape, we submit to.

Going over the specifics of political systems is beyond the scope of this book, but based on the reading I've done on the matter, I see law being more lawful when legislation is handled more by judges and juries, rather than people you vote for, who I suppose have *some* role in governance and shouldn't *all* be eliminated from office.

18. Prayer makes the world go round

Prayer is precisely how God's will works through the world. Prayers don't merely intervene in the otherwise normal course of events. Prayer to effect change *is the normal*.

It's one thing to treat prayer like a list of demands, and another to humbly petition God for something in the belief that it is in keeping with His will. My inability to tell the two apart once kept me from making petitions, thinking I was more magnanimous this way. *Oh, I don't need to ask for anything like these gullible sheep. Am I to suppose myself wiser than the maker of the heavens?* The only dignified prayer, as I saw it, was one of thanks. How inspiring it was for me to read the Platonist Ralph Waldo Emerson in his essay 'Self-reliance':

> Prayer as a means to effect a private end is meanness and theft... The prayer of the farmer kneeling in his field to weed it, the prayer of the rower kneeling with the stroke of his oar, are true prayers heard throughout nature...

The apparent humility of this naturalistic attitude concealed the mistrust I had that God answered *any* prayers. It kept me from participating actively in bringing about His goodness. I didn't realize that *God Himself* wants us to ask for things, that it is in prayers of request that we approach Him as His children, trusting in His mercy. Personal intentions aren't automatically "private ends" that merit God's disdain, but are themselves legitimate ways to bring about what God intends. Emerson, exposed to Oriental philosophies which were a novelty back in 1830s America, fashioned the self as a god of sorts, too proud to beg, only suited for sitting in contentment.

At what point does a juvenile become fully responsible for their actions? Such a question seems to make doubtful that anyone is responsible for anything really. The diversity of the ways we are conscious is a stumbling block to believe, for those who attempt to get in the mind of God in order to decide the morality, or lack thereof, of things (Genesis 3:5).

We can't presume to know God's means of judgment, only entrusting Him with the task. Some people though, in the way they were made, are unable to act with deliberation, even as adults.

And when most people reach a certain age, their grasp of reality tends to depart, and they only know they're losing it but are unable to stop the process.

I bring this up only to point out how, as certain people become or are incapable of praying for themselves or others, we bear that burden for them.

The very act of praying for those who couldn't, itself blesses the one praying, and those prayed for. The situation allows for people to rally for one another, and there are more blessings to go around precisely because of others' disadvantages. God ensures that our disabilities and sufferings are never in vain.

God hears and answers all prayers. It is never a waste to pray. If after a heartfelt prayer, the inspiration strikes to pray some more, don't stop it on account of thinking, "Oh, I just prayed already." No prayer is ever redundant. God and the saints are with you and listening, even when your mind is elsewhere as you recite from memory or some book*.

* Even not knowing the full meaning of a prayer but saying it makes it more true in your life, and that adds to faith, as you grasp the meaning of the words in relation to your widening understanding of God. The intention might come after, but it has to come.

We are assured by the Lord that we receive when we ask (Matthew 7:7). But then if we read the text surrounding that passage and its parallels (e.g. Mark 11:24; Luke 11:9; John 15:7), Jesus provides further explanation of how God the Father gives *good things*, or gives *the Holy Spirit*, and there's some business about how we need to have faith and abide in Him. Meaning, we don't necessarily receive *what we ask for*.

Are all these qualifications some cop-out by God, just so that we're not totally disappointed when things don't go as we had hoped and prayed for?

But then, God knows what we need before we ask (Matthew 6:8). The burden of meeting our needs is on His shoulders. And more important than getting what we want, is doing His will. That only requires trust on our part. And it is only in uniting our will with His will that we have the confidence of receiving that which we ask for (1 John 5:14-15). Why else would we want to ask for anything anyway?

Prayer isn't legalistic incantation where God and the saints try to trick you into saying something that puts you under their control, like some demon trickster or genie looking for a loophole in the wording you use.

God and the saints respond to your heart and not how well-worded or precise your recitation is. Like a person you're talking to in front of you, He takes what you say based on your overall disposition and not the technical merits of what you say.

When I first got in the habit of praying again, I was worried of skipping stanzas here or there, or leaving out a particular thought process that I wanted God to support. But He already knows what's in our heart before we even ask about it. What's important is that we ask.

I'd never really thought about praying "in Jesus' name," or "in the name of the Father and of the Son and of the Holy Spirit" (Matthew 28:19), until I started reading the Gospel for real in 2019. And so my prayers would include 'in Jesus' name' just as it says in John 14:13, among other verses. It took me a long while to realize I've been praying in God's name all my life, whenever I did the sign of the cross, however haphazardly, however much as a joke. How distant from God I was, I now realize, when I didn't think much of how jeepney drivers would cross themselves when passing a church by the road. That was better than my lot then, thinking I'd find happiness in money, a girl, or being heard by millions.

Our relationship with Jesus is right here, and nothing keeps Him away, even this very moment, whatever's going on in our lives. We've been confined to our homes for a year now, and what have we missed most of all? And to think, the greatest treasure, Jesus Himself, is already with us. He will be there for us no matter what happens, but we have to ask.

When I'm at my most tired or in the process of falling asleep, unable or unwilling to mouth a prayer, I make the sign of the cross, assured He is with me.

Praying for the souls in Purgatory blesses us on Earth as well. It could instill fear of Purgatory in us, in a way that we feel closer to God and can surmount temptation more easily.

In praying for these saved but still suffering souls, you're also taking time off *your* stay in Purgatory without realizing or intending it.

19. Pray for the healing of three people every night

Look for a good prayer for inner healing on the internet. I personally use the text used in Fr. Chad Ripperger's 'Deliverance prayers: For use by the laity.' Pray this for three people each night. In less than a year you'll have prayed for the healing of 1,000 people, or of several hundred people several times. That's a lot of blessings.

Even the saints had their struggles dealing with difficult people. Saint Faustina writes in her diary of the numerous times she was picked on, where her worsening tuberculosis was seen by her fellow sisters as an excuse to get out of work. This hurt Saint Faustina considerably, which I found surprising, given that she had the privilege of speaking to Jesus face to face.

We could be alright people but are just unable to deal with certain people's idiosyncrasies, or ways they cope with stress. When some people are just plain disagreeable, it helps to not just 'not judge' them, but to actually do something for them. This could include ingratiating them with favors and compliments, but I was thinking more along the lines of prayer. We could reframe offenses against our pride as someone's way of asking for help to be healed.

Praying for your enemies is not just some attempt at gaining moral high ground or to avoid 'stooping to their level.' It's about seeing another as loved by God, as someone who we could yet hope to become a saint.

20. The Bible

It seems doubtful that the books and letters that comprise the New Testament have anything to do with what Jesus really said or meant. After all, these were written decades after the fact. The tendency is to reject their literal meaning and to settle for, "This is true, figuratively at least," and insert whatever contemporary moral codes we subscribe to.

We of little faith. What Leo Tolstoy dismisses as perversions of a wise teacher's sayings were intended to be written as they are, with no 'generation loss' as could be attributable to strictly man-made works. Jesus Himself appointed the very same Apostles who either wrote or supervised the writing of what we know as the four Gospels. Where there had previously been no reason to codify His life, death, and resurrection, the Gospel and Epistles came about, to be read along with the Old Testament, and Christians since have been the beneficiaries. God knew what He was doing, and the Holy Spirit made up for the lack of education credentials of the Apostles and disciples.

Among the parts of the Gospel deemed disposable by Tolstoy was Jesus' cursing of a fig tree (Matthew 21:19; Mark 11:14), a curse that could very well be directed towards Tolstoy's fruitless "true understanding."

The more I grow in faith, the more I see how the Gospel wouldn't have had its influence on mankind if it weren't true in a very plain sense. The story of Jesus' incarnation, ministry, death, and rising from the dead wouldn't have prevailed in the 1st Century, nor yet in this one, if it weren't historically valid. It wouldn't have captured the hearts *and* minds of those who have gone to their violent deaths testifying of Jesus' divinity, if people hadn't seen His signs for themselves, and if there weren't a Holy Spirit leading people to what really happened.

But the modern tendency is to assume that it couldn't have happened in the first place (miracles = magic = impossible), and then explain with clear logical analysis in one's bubble how it's all a delusion, a lie, just a pleasant story that inspires us. Of course if it *were* true, it would be excluded from one's scope of possibilities by virtue of its apparent absurdity. To accept it would mean a reevaluation of our understanding of what could be, and what could be known of life, of us, so as to include a very personal plan for each one of us on Earth, a possibility that is not given a chance by those who, quite stubbornly, hold on to their lack of faith, however little of value this proves to be in discovering truth and the meaning of life.

The Bible

By the way, I'm not all that versed in the Bible yet. Whatever citations I give in these pages, I have to look them up. I'm very impressed by those who through their study can conjure up any verse in an instant to make whatever point they're making. That talent is not essential to knowing Him, as many Bible whizzes would admit themselves, but it makes me realize how much I overlook in my readings, and that there's so much more I have to learn.

I don't have a particular program for reading specific passages during the day. But in my reading or watching of certain topics, certain verses come up, which I like to review. I also like praying with certain parts of the Bible, particularly the Gospel, as reference.

To some extent, study and prayer with the Bible and other Christian books has distracted me from reading basically anything else. During my pagan years, I had some aspiration for 'must-reads' I had to get to eventually before death, for enrichment of my mind or something. That's over with. But it's really no problem at all. The difference between the Bible and all other 'timeless classics,' 'self-help,' and moral codes from other faiths, is that Christ is not about goodness for goodness' sake, but to know the whole point of it all: union or reunion with God through *the* way, Jesus.

21. Sacraments

Maybe you noticed, but I've been lying to you all this time. This book is *not* about 'how to be Catholic' as much as it's a defense of Church doctrine. The 'being' of it has been implied for the most part. But among the definite ways of being Catholic is the sacraments.

I'll be setting aside Matrimony, Holy Orders for priests, and Anointing of the Sick for now. And Baptism and Confirmation are also given short shrift. My main focus is on the two sacraments we should be engaging in regularly: the Holy Eucharist and Confession.

Some would object to the idea of the necessity of the sacraments in knowing our Lord, and I would ask them to pray about it. Go something like this: "O Lord, if You really did come here to save us, what means to receive Your grace did you make available for us?" Okay that's a loaded question, pointing to the sacraments as instituted by Christ Himself, but I invite you to pray on it anyway.

We have faith that God wants us to know Him. It's why He conveys His truths through words, which He specifically makes available to us in the Bible. Not only did he give us Scripture, but he founded the very institution that allows us to interpret these writings according to how He meant them to be read. This same institution, the Catholic Church, allows us to receive the grace of Christ, to bring us closer to the state humanity was in before original sin brought distance from God, and death.

Confession is rather straightforward. As with baptism, our sins are washed away, and we return to a state of grace. We find favor with God once more, and with the right resolve could fight temptations better.

I say "with the right resolve," because when confessing regularly, you may notice a pattern. For the sake of telling you about it I'll call it 'post-confession irritability,' but it might as well be 'post-confession horniness,' or maybe some issue you're struggling with. It's almost like being tested on how serious you are that you want to change. God only allows us these situations to bring us closer to Him. So after a nice, tear-filled, warm-and-fuzzy confession, expect temptations to come. They may not, but it's best to be prepared anyway.

So confession is about forgiveness. But what about the Holy Eucharist, which the Church purports to be the center of Christian life? We receive Jesus Christ, body and blood, soul and divinity, but didn't He provide for this when He died on the cross?

The way I'd explain it is, you can never have too much of Christ. You are constantly asked to sup with Him.

The mass involves a personal relationship that requires constancy not just from Jesus, Who is always there to receive you, but from you as well. Don't keep your distance from Him like, "I've accepted Him in my heart. He's already saved me. What need do I have for additional rituals? I'll just pray." That's like a husband and wife going, "Oh, no need for that sex again, we already consummated our marriage that one time." This likening of Holy Communion to Matrimony isn't incidental, with Saint Paul explaining Jesus' relationship with the Church in terms of being bridegroom to the bride (Ephesians 5:23).

Perhaps it's the eating of Jesus' body that doesn't sit well with you. It didn't sit well either with the first ones who heard Jesus talk about His being the bread of life (John 6:52;35). His critics wouldn't have objected so much if He had clarified, "Oh, that's just a metaphor."

Before Jesus even speaks of being the bread of life, we read of the miracle of His feeding the five thousand (John 6:1-15), which gives us a parallel to how He continues feeding us Catholics His body and blood in Holy Communion for two millennia now, after sacrificing Himself only once in history (Hebrews 7:27) with the Crucifixion.

When Saint Paul speaks to the Corinthians of partaking in the Eucharist in an unworthy manner, he is clearly under the impression that in the bread and drink is Jesus' actual body and blood. "For any one who eats and drinks without discerning the body eats and drinks judgment upon himself" (1 Corinthians 11:29).

All the Apostles and their appointed successors believed in Jesus' real presence in the Eucharist. Are we to argue that at some point between the Last Supper and now, this celebration became merely symbolic?

We have all this Biblical and historical evidence of the meaning of the Eucharist to early Christians, yet His real presence in the Sacred Host is still a matter of faith. It would be so much easier to subscribe to the Church's interpretation of John 6, if we saw with our own eyes His body and blood on the altar at mass. The Lord, knowing our tendency to doubt, occasionally performs a Eucharistic miracle. All Eucharists are miraculous, for sure, but I'm talking about instances where the Host actually appears as flesh and blood, and this is documented by scientists who study blood samples blindly. You can check features on YouTube for what they've found. But we're conditioned to not believe these things. Because science*.

 * As with anything scientific, the observation of Eucharistic miracles requires presumptions, since facts and empirical data do not have meaning apart from how they're interpreted. So even Eucharistic miracles require faith, that is, faith in the 2,000-year-old Church being founded by Jesus Who is God. If you believe this, then the miracles affirm your belief in

Jesus' real presence in the Eucharist. If you don't, then you will ascribe something else like demons or aliens as cause of these anomalies.

Imagine if the Host always did appear as physical flesh when blessed by the priest. How could we be assured that in spite of our unworthiness before His absolute greatness, we are happily invited to His supper? Saint Alphonsus Liguori supposes that's why the Lord remains as bread in appearance, so we aren't too intimidated or freaked out to approach Him.

But anyway, why *eat* him? Then again, why not? The Gospel tells of Jesus eating with all kinds of people. It's a way for people to form personal connections, and it's the same in Holy Communion. And the eating of Jesus the Lamb of God is also in keeping with His Jewish heritage, wherein only the unblemished lamb (Exodus 12:5; 1 Peter 1:19) could serve as a sacrifice.

If more people knew what was going on in the Eucharist, it would be held more often, with churches filled to capacity. It would be a major part of the economy, with other pressing priorities in life such as sports cars and dance clubs simply falling out of favor. Learning the significance of the parts of the mass, I now see the Eucharist as Heaven on Earth.

In Genesis 28:12, we read of Jacob dreaming of a stairway on which angels ascend and descend. At church, when we lift our hearts up to the Lord right before the consecrating of the bread and wine, the priest speaks of hosts of angels praising He who comes in the name of the Lord. This is consistent with Saint John, quoting Jesus: "Truly, truly, I say to you, you will see Heaven opened, and the angels of God ascending and descending upon the Son of man" (John 1:51). The Eucharist, in which we receive His actual body, could then be spoken of as the ladder to Heaven. If you ever felt a pull to attend mass without knowing why, this is one big reason. If ever you've been attracted to the more visibly rapturous services of other denominations, the Eucharist is the thrill you've been looking for.

    I can't pretend to have resolved all the uniqueness of the Eucharist in the preceding paragraphs. I only just started receiving the Sacred Host again after more than two decades of not doing so, and then this pandemic happened, limiting access to the Blessed Sacrament. I guess my solution for all these loose ends in my explanations is for you to pray about it. That will have to do, for what the Church herself calls a mystery.

    May I also ask you to pray for a return to normality of conditions, so that masses could be held again without restrictions? Let Jesus know that we've learned the lesson, and will never again take for granted receiving Him in the Blessed Sacrament. Thank you.

22. Obedience

At the dinner table when I was about 10, I asked my dad, "Why are we here?" and he quickly responded, "Because God loves us." I let it go at that. He may have been convinced that was why, but I wasn't.

I didn't give much credit to his answer, until I remembered it recently. Back then, it wasn't satisfying because it didn't explain why we have *this* rather than nothing at all. Perhaps it wasn't so much a reason I was looking for, as it was a finality such as I'd find in a mathematical equation or some multiple choice answer in Science class, e.g. "photosynthesis."

I don't know how much my dad pondered that question, but I can't think of a better, truer reply to give your kid, however well they grasp it, and regardless of what numbskull decisions they have yet to make before they see your point.

God as perfect and pure love is not something we appreciate often, if at all, and that's a better problem to concern ourselves with rather than something that simply manages to satisfy our curiosity.

Obedience

As a rebel away from Christ, I didn't want to be subject to some external voice telling me what to do. I likened the very idea of religion as some reality show doing what some uptight 'other' wanted, where people were made to act with no inner validation or conviction. The devil and 'sin' were just bogeymen used to scare the masses into submission, making people ashamed to do things that were actually perfectly healthy or at least harmless. It was a racket, and I wasn't buying.

To get to that amoral way of thinking, I had to have given up faith that there is a God bigger than any of us. That's where the problem lay. Now that I'm back in the Church, I see how He knows what's good for me better than I do. My obedience is precisely the way He takes care of me.

Hearing the term 'God's glory' never did much for me. It sounds like the Almighty beating His chest and for what? Our adulation? When 'Glory to God in the highest' would come up in the mass, my attitude, even after my return to the Church was, "And then what? How does that serve anybody, that God is glorified?"

And the Jesuit motto "For the greater glory of God" likewise invites a retort of, "And then what?"

We take glory as a puffing up of ego, but this comes from our human frame of reference, where we associate glory with achieving 'great' things for one's self, or one's country, and the like. Such glory isn't wrong in itself, but it has to acknowledge that all we accomplish comes from God alone.

Glory in the context of God is free of our worldly associations. In the Bible, the glory of God is often associated with a more intimate knowledge of Him, in what we'd call mystical experiences. Saint Paul says, "The glory of the celestial is one, and the glory of the terrestrial is another" (1 Corinthians 15:40). His glory is not for Him alone, but for all of us.

I suppose some of our grievances, doubts, and even apathy about the Bible and Catholicism in general has to do with reorienting our way of thinking about a lot of the terms we hear being thrown around, such as 'glory' here, and 'jealous God' as explained above in Chapter 3. The remedy isn't so much about updating some Biblical glossary, as it is a call to open ourselves to what He's telling us personally.

If I am to fall from my renewed faith, perhaps a year from now, maybe decades later, I suppose it would be out of weariness of trying to live up to Jesus' perfect example. In my frailty, I would conclude that rigid Catholicism was one end of the devil's extremes, the other end being mindless, anything-goes hedonism. "What moderate pleasures I've missed!" I would muse. And for what? In order to suck up to some dictator deity whose reality I was convinced of from the tales of malnourished, schizophrenic saints? I would lament the friends that one by one fell off from my life, who would then see in me only the shadow of

Obedience

the fun-for-the-most-part guy they used to know before "that Catholic thing" made me go off the deep end. Wouldn't it be nice to just live a little at last?...

Or maybe, I could keep up the Christian 'keywords' and rhetoric, and no one will know the difference when I begin skipping and later abandoning altogether my prayers, in the end more of a bothersome chore. No one will know I've gone back to my sinful ways, and my conscience, what remains of it, will rest easy in knowing I tried and just couldn't cut it. I'm pretty sure that's what many rogue clergy go through, when they give up the fight against smart satan.

I look at the possibility above and it's hard to say with conviction that I'll always submit to our Lord Jesus Christ and honor Mother Mary. That's scary. For all the devotion I've promised of myself, I'm still a long way from feeling assured of the salvation of Christ. And I presume to bring more people into the faith by writing this thing you're holding! Whatever happens, you can't say the Lord didn't give me every opportunity to turn away from my faithlessness.

But then, Thomas à Kempis in 'The imitation of Christ' tells us to be on guard for temptation, as long as we live. smart satan will try to sway us with emotion, reason, fear of being misunderstood, hunger... Just anything that will wear us down into forgetting that every action has its implications, and is known and felt by God.

More dreadful than sinning though, is not trusting in His mercy, thinking we could do without

Him, forgetting that His yoke is easy and burden light (Matthew 11:30).

I guess it's good to not be overconfident of my salvation. At the very least, it keeps me on guard against the wickedness and snares of the devil. Whatever nagging doubts I have, I know in my heart Jesus isn't just a wise teacher, or a really good guy, or a mythical ideal. No other but God could have reached me as He has. For the rest of this life, nothing will keep me from His love (Romans 8:38-39). All I have to do is ask.

23. The Philippines

Being born and raised in the Philippines never meant much to me, other than that the food, both local and fused, was the best. I would even characterize myself as not being nationalistic. When watching movies in cinemas or attending conferences where the national anthem was played, I'd make an effort to not be in the room, just to avoid standing then.

But I know now that God intended my country as a spiritual 'oasis' in the Pacific. Thanks to special historical circumstances, the country is 80% Roman Catholic, at least nominally, in contrast to most of Asia. Catholicism here is almost something to take for granted. In sharing the Gospel to Filipinos, you're not telling them something they haven't heard before or have no idea about. In one way, that's a disadvantage. However, having Catholic tradition as a kind of default mode also makes it so much easier to reform, as I did. When I started actually caring about practicing my Christianity, I didn't have to enroll in some initiation process, waiting for months to be baptized. In fact, when I was ready to accept Christ I was already confirmed, even though back when I was a teen, Confirmation was little more than an excuse to order good food. The point being, the sacraments are relatively easy to come by, whenever you get around to asking for them.

I often hear gripes — mostly from the *wiser*, more well-to-do elite — of the Filipino people having bad work habits and attitudes, and voting for inept and corrupt politicians that keep the country from achieving greater economic progress. There may be more than a grain of truth here, but also, look at all the progress in the so-called first world that is quickly abandoning all pretense of religiosity, in favor of what they call freedom but what is more aptly termed licentiousness.

Even with all the corruption we read about in the headlines, and the hypocrisy and lukewarmness of leaders from whom we're supposed to look for guidance, faith continues to be a huge part of Filipinos' lives in a way it isn't in most other places. Up until recently, the '3 o'clock habit' was something we knew about from local TV to commemorate the hour of Jesus' death, with the guy with the deep imposing voice reciting, "Holy God, Holy Mighty One, Holy Immortal One, Have mercy on us and on the whole world." Indeed, to be Filipino is to be #blessed.

All things are possible through God (Matthew 19:26), but I don't know how I would have returned to the Church if it weren't for my upbringing and environment. I barely got back as it is. If I'm still to wonder why God put me in this country, this is the reason.

COMING HOME

24. My conversion

The whole story of converting, or returning to the faith of my childhood, is more encompassing than could be told here, and the process of renewal continues to this day. I'll try to spare you details in giving an overview of how finding Jesus happened even after treating him as a basically inconsequential part of life since my teens.

One important thing that I may have underestimated at the time was that I was around people who took their Catholic faith seriously. When I had pretty much relegated the Gospel to an ancient document consisting of instructive fairy tales, I knew of these smart people taking Jesus as true, and not in the 'enlightened' allegorical way I did, but believing that in this man from the Middle East *literally* lay our salvation, the very meaning of life.

With all the concerns of modern adulthood, He just wasn't an issue. I'd maybe give Him token props as a source of inspiration, but not as Someone to revolve my life around.

This period of my life was from around 1997 to 2018, with cracks in this rather reasonable way of thinking beginning to show in the years leading up to converting.

What may have softened up my intellectual position without my realizing it at the time, preparing me to eventually take a leap of faith, was music. Back in the 1990s, heavy metal served as an emotionally rewarding substitute to the dull Bible and sacraments which I rebelled against, but around 2014, in a kind of reversal of the process, I got into sacred choral music in a big way, specifically J.S. Bach's B minor mass. I may have thought it was just my musical boundaries that were being expanded, but how fortuitous that such aesthetic stimulation would happen with a piece where the words "*Kyrie eleison*" ("Lord have mercy") are sung repeatedly for over 10 minutes. Bach himself was inspired to complete the mass just a couple of years before his death, even though as a Lutheran, the distinctly Roman Catholic form of the composition was somewhat foreign to him. It wouldn't be a total surprise for me to find out in the afterlife that *part* of the reason the Holy Spirit moved Bach to assemble his masterpiece was to reach a proud boy, me, 370 years into the future.

The hard thing about turning away from a merely mythological view of Christ is that He appears here as just one of many choices for learning moral values, values of which pagans can get behind, out of sheer practicality. It is prudent and it feels good to be kind to others, and people are less likely to take offense at and hurt you. Not recognizing Jesus as the source of all goodness, doesn't mean there aren't advantages, both in the short term and in the long term, in being a good person. It is a satisfying position to be in, one in which a pursuit of the divine is often not in consideration. What's more, you may know people of other faiths who get by quite well in their being good people, and that gives the impression that there is nothing particularly unique about any one religion.

I would consume books and podcasts of a philosophical bent, and I guess even then I was looking for more of an answer to life than whatever I had back then. Three authors served as steps in my return to Christ: Immanuel Kant, Julian Jaynes, and Søren Kierkegaard. Kant and Jaynes weren't even Christian, but spoke of Christ as a herald of a new consciousness in which morals became increasingly a matter of inwardness — of the heart — rather than outward action alone. The implicit assumption here was that morality was something evolved into, not something bestowed by a God, much less a loving one.

Jaynes, most known for his bicameral theory that places the dawn of conscious man at just around 3,000 years ago, is a weird intellectual influence of mine. Through him, I realized that whatever 'truths' science provided us, were abstractions separate from living. Direct experience, in which the reality of our being here is self-evident, was something else altogether. Jaynes never even said these things in his writings. He died thinking that religion had been superseded by science, and that discovering the origin of consciousness was a matter of scientific discovery, rather than a spiritual one. So I'm convinced of the Holy Spirit's role in removing any hope of mine that science was a way to obtain answers that matter, because Jaynes sure didn't say this.

Kant, on the other hand, says that we could never know anything for certain, but only what things appear to be. This immediately rejects our being made in God's image (Genesis 1:27), and our capacity to discover an ultimate purpose to things*. Still, his high-minded rhetoric of treating people as ends in themselves, helped me recognize the dignity of people apart from whatever use they were to me.

* Kant spoke of religion but only "within the boundaries of mere reason," the very title of one of his books. His skepticism over what could be known of existence makes it clear that he remained an unbeliever, for if he truly accepted that we are made in God's image, then he would have given more credence to what God reveals to us in our temporal existence.

In my faithless years, Kierkegaard was a puzzle to me, because philosophers seemed to take him, a Christian, seriously. When my experience with Jaynes helped me see direct experience as something distinct from science, the title of one of Kierkegaard's books, 'Concluding unscientific postscript,' got my attention. When I finally got around to reading it, I thought I was just going to get an affirmation of what I already believed, but instead, Kierkegaard, or at least his pseudonym Johannes Climacus, mused on how a relationship with the historical Jesus Christ could be the means to eternal happiness. After thinking so symbolically of Christ for so long, I couldn't go that far. But at least I became on the lookout for the 'paradox-religious' involving Christ, as Kierkegaard

My conversion

described. Even when I couldn't believe, I *wanted* to believe.

Getting closer to finding and accepting the truth wasn't a matter of doing one thing or another specifically. These were just God's way of bringing me back to Him. Each event was part of a causal chain to get to my subsequent acceptance of Jesus, but it was the Holy Spirit transforming me.

In the middle of 2019, I underwent neurofeedback therapy, which supposedly allows for better management of one's emotions and behaviors, through regulation of brainwaves. It's said to be of particular help to special needs kids and stroke patients, but these are health benefits, nothing particularly spiritual. In my case, I think it helped me concentrate on tasks, made it easier to get into a productive groove, and facilitated my learning of new things. If I was to relate this to my later conversion, I might surmise that my mind was opened to new spiritual possibilities, but if so, it's only because God planned it that way, and not because of any unique features of the therapy.

Around the same time, I encountered a book by Caroline Myss that purported to explain the writings of Saint Teresa of Avila, whose mysticism I was a fan of even as an unbeliever. One thing Myss encouraged was prayer, something I hadn't done for so long apart from a vague 'Thank you' in times of relief. Myss probably meant prayer in terms of communication with some mysterious source of infinite wisdom by which we advance in spirituality, rather than the nurturing of a personal relationship with Jesus Christ. Jesus, to her, is just one of many spiritual guides to choose from, essentially no different from the Buddha and other "masters" of the major spiritual traditions. Still, the connection with an actual saint of the Church, however misrepresented by Myss' archetypal psycho-babble, was enough of an opening for me to eventually return to the one true Son of God.

It's a wonder I even picked up Myss' book, having read my share of New Age books back in college, and dismissing them as mostly harmless superstition. Since returning to the faith, however, I don't think the New Age is as benign as all that. This 50-year-old 'new' movement, with its Hinduistic-Buddhistic bent, presents another 'way' to God other than Jesus, and must be rejected as yet another variant of the heresies of Simon Magus (Acts 8:9), misdirecting the faithful away from the gifts of the Church, particularly the Eucharist and proper interpretation of Scripture.

Even in such confusion, the Holy Spirit freed me. This is what convinces me that God will always reach you, amid whatever sin and falsehood you cling to, if you ask. Sometimes, even if you don't. The particular circumstance by which God carries the message of His truth is only incidental, not essential.

My conversion

My initial prayer, of "Lord, may I be ever more aware of Your presence" is generic enough to not be about Jesus, but it was enough to be graced by Him. Less than a couple of months after occasionally reciting it, on September 4, 2019, it occurred to me that if there really is a God, He would make Himself known to us His creations. And that Jesus, on whom history itself is centered, could very well have done what He is said to have done — namely, rise from the dead — because *He* is God. That was when I finally said, "Yes, of course!"

From that night onward, my interest grew. There was still a lot of intellectual-emotional baggage that diverted my attention from Jesus as God Himself, but the important thing was that I wanted to know more.

Since then, the only books I read have to do with Jesus, with a couple of exceptions in which someone recommended a book to me, but I'm increasingly less inclined to humor others in this way. All my previous literary favorites are as good as trash to me now. For instance, I used to consider a book of Ralph Waldo Emerson's essays as my 'desert island' book. I could no longer stand his empty, flowery verbosity. The insistence on treating even spiritual realities as neat allegory is the poet's downfall.

And lest my discovery of Jesus' true divinity become yet another point of pride, God willed that of all people, Kanye West would release an album at the same time proclaiming the same message that 'Jesus is King.' "Whatever truths you're learning," I could remind myself, "Kanye got there first." Indeed, my conversion is not an isolated case. David Garrison's book 'A wind in the house of Islam' tells of a mass conversion of Muslims who encounter Jesus in their dreams, and He reveals Himself as God, not a mere prophet as the Koran maintains. If Jesus could reach those who otherwise would have nothing to do with the Gospel, what more baptized Christians who have simply strayed over time?

It's one thing to believe in Christ, it's another thing to avail of the fruits of His ministry on Earth. I was praying more than I ever had, and would even visit a chapel frequently. The first two times I entered the chapel, I was moved to tears within the first few seconds of sitting. I told myself as a reflex that it was just me being oversentimental and happening to be in physical pain. But of course it was the Holy Spirit. Those true moments are His.

Being new to conversion, the sacraments, particularly the mass, seemed like something *other* Christians would do when their faith is reduced to going through the motions. But while meditating during All Saints' Day 2019, it occurred to me so matter of factly that my relationship with others was a *real* thing. We really are united by the Holy Spirit, in a way that couldn't be broken, however distant another may be. And the song 'One bread, one body,' based on Saint Paul's words in 1 Corinthians 10:17, made sense for the first time in my life.

This may sound elementary, something a child could intuitively grasp, but it was a big deal to me on account of all the philosophy I had studied that told me otherwise, stuff like no one ever truly seeing blue in the same way, or that what we take to be connection with another is the most fleeting of collisions, like two circles meeting at only one point. The whole time I fashioned each of us as islands bridged only by the coincidental agreement of metaphorical language, I neglected to consider the earth underneath even the deepest of waters. What skepticism lacks is the assurance of a God who out of love reveals Himself to us, making us all brothers and sisters.

So I went to church. The Gospel reading for that day ended with, "For the Son of man came to seek and to save the lost" (Luke 19:10). I didn't hear the priest read it then, though; I underestimated the parking problem and only arrived in church at around the homily. Such a newbie.

Attending the Eucharist once more, and actually looking forward to it for the first time in my life, was a big step. But even then, the notion of eating the actual flesh and blood of Jesus wasn't something I had accepted in full, though I'd say "Amen" when receiving Him. And it would take a little more convincing that the Roman Catholic Church, which I was so conveniently baptized into since infancy, was *the* Church. But that would come in time, just as I would find out that I should have gone to Confession prior to the Eucharist, since my soul was in a state of mortal sin after so many years away from the Lord. In my first Confession in over 20 years, the priest referred to my return as a "grace," and I thought, "So it is." And I've been using the word 'grace' ever since, as you may have noticed throughout this book.

I had a Crucifix my mom had given me in my teens, which I would only wear as an ornament when going out. The extra weight on my neck just seemed too much of an inconvenience when I was home and wanted to relax. But soon after that first mass, I began wearing it more regularly. I was similarly inspired to put on a Miraculous Medal I had first noticed lying around years ago. I had no idea what it was. The text on the medal was so small, I had to use the zoom of my camera to read the letters, 'REGINA SINE LABE ORIGINALI CONCEPTA O.P.N.' Googling the Latin ("Queen conceived without original sin, pray for us"), I found out there was a whole tradition connected to it. That medal was the beginning of me really noticing Mother Mary's guidance in my life. One morning nine months later, I woke up to see that the clasp in which the medal was housed, was wide open, and I could no longer find it. Wherever it is, I hope that it is blessing the persons in its vicinity.

Why this roundaboutness only to arrive at the truth? In fifth grade, I remember I couldn't even go to sleep without saying "God" as my last word, in case I died that night.

As much as it hurt Him, I know God willed it all along. I wouldn't have made such an effort to develop my talents, if it weren't for a pagan intensity. That sounds heretical, I know, like God approving of such a lifestyle, but it does shed light on why humanity isn't equally given His graces throughout history, why some cultures and nations are permitted by divine providence to be less in His favor. A certain sharpening of worldly ability serves as a slingshot or catapult, for His name to be carried off to yet farther reaches of the world*. In my case, I managed to get fairly proficient with music**, political economy, and brushing teeth, among other things, in a way I wouldn't have if I had been comforted by the meaning of life, i.e. Jesus, beforehand. And if all that crap over the past two decades was in order to write this little book and reach those who may need it, then it will all be worth it, detours and all.

* Which begs the question of, why not just reveal Himself to us in equal measure already? We have to content ourselves that that's just His way. Sorry folks!

** I look back and see how my experiences from listening to music have prepared me for prayer. The most enriching moments are those in which I don't approach an activity for the sake of feeling good or spiritual consolation. It is in letting go of preconceptions and expectations that emotional rewards come more easily, and even then they are a secondary concern. Kind of Zen, but without the nothing.

Upon my return to the Church, I thought my faith was to be sustained by, well, faith. I knew that all of science gave no *meaning* to life, and so when people would speak of evidence of an afterlife or give their testimonies of encountering Jesus in person, my tendency was to downplay these with, "It may all be true, but I'm not willing to place my belief on things that could be falsified. Faith is beyond asking for proof, and that's good enough for me." But more and more I became convinced of these supernatural things happening throughout history, such as in Fatima and Lourdes. As a pagan, I may have heard about the Shroud of Turin, but it was only as a believer that I found out how modern science was stumped as to its features. And I'd never really known what Our Lady of Guadalupe was about, but I soon enough learned about the apparent impossibility of the 500-year-old tilma, for which no one has explanations. Sherlock Holmes' adage of eliminating the impossible in order to arrive at the truth however improbable, doesn't work when what is possible and impossible couldn't even be established. Unless you're willing to believe a secret organization has managed to fool the public by replacing the tilma every so often so as to account for its perfect condition centuries later, and all the facts we've been told about it, such as the images of people within the eye of Our Lady, are based on forged documents and false testimonies, all this hushed up for 500 years now. Or maybe aliens would be an easier truth to swallow. With the public's penchant for conspiracy theories, especially against the Church, we would have heard a good refutation of Guadalupe and many other Church-approved miracles by now, if there was one.

The reality of the divine, specifically of Jesus Christ as God, opens up only *after* embracing the faith, almost like a reward for believing without seeing. I wonder: If I had encountered such evidence before I was ready to accept Christ, how would I have wiggled my way out of simply believing? What flimsy explanations would I have hung onto? Perhaps mass delusions? Corrupt scientists? My entire life being a reality show and the audience laughing at my cluelessness? Anything to avoid the fact that my understanding of the world was severely limited unless I accepted a personal God and Savior, the same one my parents told me about when I was a toddler. How unclimactic can you get?

25. You found Jesus; now what?

On the internet, I read of former Catholics with their vile, snide, and sometimes sensible remarks about their experiences growing up and questioning things, much of which I could relate to, but I can't pretend to know *all* their pain or to have the answer to *all* their grievances. Nothing of what I say could bring you closer to Him, without His grace. In this book, I've tried to take into account the major objections and reservations about the faith, but after I'm done blabbing, it's His call on whether you find what you've been seeking. But I'll try to be of some help.

This chapter is in the event you come to a similar conclusion as mine, that Christ is God, and the Bible and the Eucharist are His revelations to guide our moral lives.

When first saying "Yes" to the truth that is Jesus, don't *expect* understanding. That's not the point of telling people about your experience. You leave a door open, and it's not up to you if another steps through it.

The general consensus will be "Good for you," in the sense of, "It's good to have *something* to believe in." That's the language of one who has yet to say "Yes," and that's okay. Again, it's a matter of grace. We speak of finding Jesus, but the reality is He finds us.

Meanwhile, offer yourself as a resource for any questions others may have, while acknowledging that you yourself are still in the process of inner conversion. Every Catholic is undergoing conversion until they die.

When this Jesus freakishness gets more serious, your priorities will rearrange without much effort. You'll still have your obligations. Contrary to the impression I'm making, being Catholic isn't about watching Catholic shows all day but actually serving others with your unique talents. However, you will find your time being freed up, time that you once spent on social media, political gossip, i.e. current events, and entertainment, which I discussed in Chapter 16.

As I am learning to see the world with new eyes, I've become rather particular. Some would say judge-y. I'm more mindful of the impression I make on others, and whether I'm condoning other people's behavior for things I wouldn't have bothered about before, such as exclamations using God's name*. I'm not always sure if I should speak up or just wait for the Lord to make others more disposed to receive Him.

* I never understood why this would be second among the 10 Commandments, until I realized that the way we say God's name, whether with reverence and intention or without, reflects our relationship with Him. We make it much harder to call on

Him sincerely in our time of need, when in more comfortable times we treat His name as nothing more than a really handy expression.

You'll find that in the Catholisphere, as in most other places, there is a tendency to label people as their actions. We're not supposed to judge (Matthew 7:1), much less reduce people to particular sins in our judgment.

Being more discerning as to the wrongs of the world doesn't equate to gossip about others as a way of making right these wrongs. You have to recognize smart satan's method of trying to pull you back into the world. You can be more mindful of the company you keep, without rejecting others because of the current way they live.

It's good to estimate how receptive people are to you at a given moment. You may be tempted to go over the whole Catechism with them, but something as small as saying a prayer in their company could bear eternal fruit and make a greater impression.

And it's not like you're automatically a holy saint from now on either. Take care that you don't fall back into your previous wicked habits just because certain behaviors are so prevalent to the point of seeming 'not a big deal.'

As your interest in all things Catholic grows, you're going to encounter people on the Web who call themselves Catholics, whom I'd rather call 'pleasant dinner guests.' They're the ones who brandish a laundry list of other people's offenses in order to judge them. "So you're divorced. You're going to Hell. So you receive Communion on the hand. You're going to Hell. So you believe in gay marriage. You're going to Hell. So we don't get along. You're going to Hell..." You get the idea*. More likely than not, they don't even recognize the present pope as pope, even though Jesus Himself did say that the gates of Hell would not prevail over the Church founded on Saint Peter (Matthew 16:18). By their standards, *they're* going to Hell.

* While we are guided in our understanding of right and wrong, we could never know enough of another's situation to replace the Lord as judge during His second coming.

They may pray the Rosary, or at least tell people to pray the Rosary, and have an assortment of holy images and statues and Crucifixes to decorate their homes and offices. They may even make good sense on certain theological issues that most in the faith know little of. That's smart satan's trickery, like a politician who likes to invoke "God" or whatever a more acceptable buzzword is today, who may even cry on camera as needed to get votes.

Remember that these pleasant dinner guests don't speak for Catholics, and don't be too disheartened seeing the splinters in the Church. That just means you're more needed to share His word than you thought. Everyone needs to be prayed for, especially the jerks.

For most of my life, I was a much worse Christian than most of you, yet here I am asking you to be more faithful. That brash righteousness only comes from a real transformation effected by the very presence of Someone, Whom we're beginning to hope is all love, the only one we couldn't do without. The last thing I want you to take away, if I haven't spelled it out yet, may be the most important message, that God is love, and Jesus, God Himself, loves you completely.

26. A rebel's prayer

Lord, please let me know You are with me.

If You are the answer to all things in life, I am sorry that as of yet, I could not acknowledge this.

Please grant me more time on this Earth, long enough to know the truth. May I not abuse this kindness by prolonging my engagement in frivolous things.

You seem really important to those who sincerely believe in You, and I know them to be alright people. If You are Who they say You are, please heal the hurts of my heart, as I know You want to. May the day come when I can humbly approach You, with You at my side without delay.

I thank You for Your patience. Amen.

ACKNOWLEDGMENTS

I'd like to thank those who prayed for my return to the faith. I know my mother Telly did. And anyone else who saw my sorry condition once and said, "Bless him!" or "May God teach you some manners!" or who said a Rosary, this is what you get.

To my favorite adult person, you don't know how much easier it is to love others because of you. Will tell you about the past few years if you have the time.

Also to the next generation and the succeeding ones, thank you for giving me a reason to write these things. Please stay literate.

ABOUT

Paul How is based in the Philippines. He recently returned to university, in order to better dumb down his words for the academe. He thinks it's still sometimes okay to hug, if you keep things clean, i.e. disinfected, using mainly a tap of arms, and don't breathe on each other. This doesn't constitute medical advice and is his personal opinion.

He pretends to give biographical information in the 'About' page but mostly just rambles his way through. One true thing though is that he is already planning his next project, based on his new favorite genre, conversion testimonies. If you have a story or know someone with a story that you think would be a good addition to his intended collection, please send an e-mail to paul@paulspurpose.com. Don't worry that what you have to say might be too dull, or about making stuff up. Everything will be screened anyway. Non-Catholic believers in Christ are welcome to share as well; ultimately, we're all Catholics in the making. If you don't have a testimony in mind and just want to complain or debate about something he said in this book, feel free to write.

Printed in Great Britain
by Amazon